DID SOMEONE YOU LOVE DIE?

DID SOMEONE YOU LOVE DIE?

Tracy A. Philips

GUILT

HEALING

GRIEVING

DEPRESSION

ADJUSTMENT

DENIAL

ACCEPTANCE

Enslow Publishing
101 W. 23rd Street
Suite 240
New York, NY 10011
USA

enslow.com

Published in 2016 by Enslow Publishing, LLC
101 W. 23rd Street, Suite 240, New York, NY 10011

Library of Congress Cataloging-in-Publication Data

Philips, Tracy A.
  Did someone you love die? / Tracy A. Philips.
    pages cm. — (Got issues?)
  Includes bibliographical references and index.
  Summary: "Discusses problems and difficulties facing those who are grieving, including symptoms and ways to help"—Provided by publisher.
  ISBN 978-0-7660-6985-5
  1. Grief in adolescence—Juvenile literature. 2. Grief—Juvenile literature. 3. Loss (Psychology) in adolescence. 4. Loss (Psychology)—Juvenile literature. I. Title.
  BF724.3.G73P523 2016
  155.9'37—dc23
                      2015011774

Printed in the United States of America

To Our Readers: We have done our best to make sure all Web site addresses in this book were active and appropriate when we went to press. However, the author and the publisher have no control over and assume no liability for the material available on those Web sites or on any Web sites they may link to. Any comments or suggestions can be sent by e-mail to customerservice@enslow.com.

Portions of this book originally appeared in the book *Losing Someone You Love: Dealing With Death and Dying.*

Disclaimer: For many of the images in this book, the people photographed are models. The depictions do not imply actual situations or events.

Contents

Everyone Experiences Loss

Most people will experience a loss at some point during their lifetime. This loss can be the death of a family member, friend, coworker, teacher, or even an acquaintance. Unfortunately, some people will experience this loss at a young age. This creates emotions and feelings that may be new to the young person, and they may not know how to handle them. This also means those caring for the young person need to understand how to best offer support for the grief they are experiencing. Young people are still developing both physically and emotionally during adolescence. Understanding how grief can impact a young person is important, as it helps family members, professionals, and friends help the person through this turbulent time and help them cope with their loss. It is important for those close to the grieving person to be supportive and nonjudgmental. It is also important to see signs that indicate the person may be in need of professional help.

Physical and Emotional Reactions

Grief is a natural response to loss. As humans, we grieve the loss of a loved one, the loss of a friend, the loss of a pet, the loss of a job, the loss of security, the loss of a cherished possession, and even the loss of a game. Each person experiences grief in a unique way. However, there are responses that are common to many people grieving the loss of a loved one. These responses are an indication of the emotional states that many grieving people go through at some point during their sadness. It can be helpful for teens to have knowledge of the emotions related to grief when trying to help others or to cope with a loss themselves.

The grieving process can affect a person physically, as well as emotionally. It is common for a person who is grieving to have changes in sleep patterns, appetite, and even personality. The person may have increased anxiety and may have difficulty concentrating. These strong emotions can be overwhelming.

The loss of someone close is difficult regardless of a person's age. However, teens are especially vulnerable to emotional turmoil when dealing with the loss of a loved one. Teens may not have been exposed to death before, and as a result, some may feel a sense of indestructibility, as if nothing can stop them or hurt them. Teens may have assumed that their friend or family member would always be there for them. If that person dies, the shock and grief can be devastating. It is important for the people in a grieving teen's life to continue to keep the lines of communication open, to be there for him or her, and to talk about these new feelings if he or she is ready to talk. A grieving teen should never have to feel isolated.

How to Help

It can be a bit awkward to spend time with someone who is grieving, as it is often hard to know what to say. People may feel helpless in the situation. However, just being there for someone and offering support can be extremely helpful.

If you don't know what to say to a grieving friend, just offer a sympathetic ear. People who are grieving often just need someone who will listen to them.

One of the most important things that someone can do for a grieving friend or family member is to offer to listen. Letting a person talk about the loss can help. If the grieving person wants it, activities such as going to the mall or playing video games can help take his or her mind off things.

It is important that people do not distance themselves from grieving teens or treat them differently. Although change is going on in their lives, they need some things that are constant. Being treated differently by a friend or family member may make them feel like an outcast and contribute to their grief.

The Impact of Loss

Humans have strong emotional connections to each other and strong relationships with one another. The loss of a loved one or friend can cause a void in a person's life—a void that may never be filled. Each person has a unique relationship with each person they hold close, and people act differently in different relationships. One person may be a responsible daughter to her parents but a fun-loving and carefree companion to her best friend. When there is a loss of that relationship due to death or illness, people may suffer depression or a sense of hopelessness because someone they identified with—someone who was a part of them—is now gone. Now there is emptiness and a loss of a part of themselves in a sense. The grieving person now needs to find ways to find enjoyment again in life, and sometimes they may need help working through their emotions and feelings of loss and grief.

Coping

There is a lot going on in the days and weeks after a death. Often the house is full of people. Friends bring food, stop by to offer condolences, and check in to see how the family of the deceased is doing. There are arrangements to be made for a funeral or memorial service. Sometimes these distractions help those who are grieving. They have something to focus their attention on. It is when all of

Losing a family member can create a void in the lives of the survivors. Because that relationship is gone, the survivor may feel that a part of him or her is gone, as well.

A Poem About Loss

"The Widower" is a poem written by Rudyard Kipling. It demonstrates the unending love between a husband and wife, even in the presence of death.

For a season there must be pain—
For a little, little space
I shall lose the sight of her face,
Take back the old life again
While she is at rest in her place.

For a season this pain must endure,
For a little, little while
I shall sigh more often than smile
Till Time shall work me a cure,
And the pitiful days beguile.

For that season we must be apart,
For a little length of years,
Till my life's last hour nears,
And, above the beat of my heart,
I hear Her voice in my ears.

But I shall not understand—
Being set on some later love,
Shall not know her for whom I strove,
Till she reach me forth her hand,
Saying, "Who but I have the right?"
And out of a troubled night
Shall draw me safe to the land.

this stops—the funeral is over, the neighbors do not stop by as often to check in—that it becomes quiet. For some grieving people, this may be the first time the loss truly hits them.

It is important for those who are grieving to understand that these feelings of emptiness are not uncommon. If a loved one is gone, it is okay to feel a loss. To not feel a loss might indicate that the person is in denial. Sometimes people try to ignore what they don't understand or what scares them.

Some people try to block out memories of the person who is now gone, as thinking of him or her is too painful. Conversely, other people become obsessed with the loss and tend to stay focused on the past rather than on the present or future. Some people feel guilty. They may think of times that they were not as kind as they feel they should have been to the person who is now gone. It is nearly impossible to have a close and strong relationship with a person and not have at least a few regrets about something said or done.

Focus on the Positive

Sometimes the guilt over past actions is painful. A person might think, "If only I had told him I loved him," or "If only I had walked home with him, he would not have been in that car accident and would be alive today." It is not healthy to stay focused on those types of thoughts, as the if onlys will only create more despair. It is impossible to change the past, and staying focused on the past takes away from focusing on the present and getting through each day. It is important to focus on the positive parts of the relationship and the happy memories. All people make mistakes. Every close relationship has its good times and its bad times. It is important not to focus on the bad times.

Each relationship has its place in a person's life. People have different kinds of bonds with grandparents than with their parents, for example. When a death alters that relationship, other issues may arise that the grieving person did not foresee. For example, the loss of a parent brings feelings of sadness but also feelings of insecurity.

Children may feel frightened for the future, as one of their primary caregivers is now gone. They may have fear that the surviving parent will die, as well, and that then they will be an orphan.[1] When a husband loses a wife, he may feel that his partner in life is gone, and he may fear going through life alone, sad, and wondering if he will ever be truly happy again.

Each loss carries with it unique feelings and emotions. The loss of a pet can be devastating. After all, pets can be humans' best friends. However, the feelings of sadness may not be the same type of sadness that people experience when they lose their parent or grandparent. For each unique personal relationship people have as family members, there are unique issues surrounding that loss. In this book, each chapter will explore the unique relationships teens have with their friends, family members, and pets and the emotional ties involved in each relationship. This book's purpose is to provide a better understanding of these issues so people will be able to offer support and guidance to grieving friends and family and will know where to look for help with their own grief. This book explores the support options that are available to teens and the need for counseling and support from peers going through a similar situation. It will cover the signs of grief and how to know when teens may be in need of professional help to deal with their grief issues.

Grief's Impact

Over the years, there has been a great deal of research about the grieving process and how to understand the emotions of those who have suffered a loss. Questions regarding the person's mental state and possible depression have arisen in the past several years. Recently the Diagnostic and Statistical Manual of Mental Disorders made some changes to the diagnostic criteria associated with grief. The DMS-5 is the fifth edition of the book used by health care professionals. It is what they reference when they diagnose a person with a mental health issue. The first edition was published in 1952, and the fifth edition was released in May 2013. Over the years, the book has been revised to include new diagnoses, update criteria for diagnoses already included, and in some cases eliminate diagnoses from the book.

Changes were made in the latest edition to address grief and depression. These are important changes, as they help health professionals understand what to look for when deciding if a person's responses to grief are healthy or connected to depression. With prior editions of this manual, health care providers were advised not to diagnose major depression in people are within two months of losing a loved one. This was called the bereavement exclusion.[1] Since the new edition was released in 2013, this exclusion was removed, as it is now believed that grief does not insulate a person from major depression. Hopefully, this will prevent clinicians from overlooking major depression in a grieving person. This was a major change, and it does represent this changing field of study. As more data becomes available with research, theories will change or expand to include this new research.

Does Everyone Grieve the Same Way?

One cannot discuss grief without discussing Elisabeth Kübler-Ross's stages of grief, as her work was influential in the study of grief responses. Kübler-Ross was a psychiatrist who developed five different stages to describe the ways in which people deal with grief. Even though there has been research to expand on these ideas or even counter them, the five stages of grief are utilized by many professionals in the mental health field to help people cope with loss and grief. These stages were initially used to describe people who were coming to terms with a terminal illness.

The theory consists of the following stages: denial, anger, bargaining, depression, and acceptance.

Denial. Denial is a defense mechanism. It is a way of either consciously or unconsciously refusing to accept certain facts. When told of devastating news, a person may initially react with disbelief and insist that the person who gave the news must be mistaken. This is the mind's way of initially rejecting information that may be too painful to accept at that time. When a person comes out of the denial phase, the reality of the situation can be devastating. He or she is left with having to figure out a way to deal with the intense emotions of sadness and despair.

The Kübler-Ross Stages of Grief

This graph illustrates psychiatrist Elisabeth Kübler-Ross's five stages of grief and how a person may experience a roller coaster of emotions over time. Each individual may go through the stages in a different order, experience several of them at the same time, or skip some altogether.

Anger. Once people come to grips with the reality of a situation, such as the death of a loved one, they may get angry. This anger may be directed at God, at a person who could be responsible for their grief, or at anyone available to assign blame. Sometimes people are even angry with the person who died. Why didn't he wear his seat belt? Why did she have to smoke when she knew she could get cancer? It is important for the person to try to deal with anger in a healthy manner.

For example, the parents of a murdered child suffer through grief that most people cannot understand. The anger associated with such a senseless and brutal murder can destroy lives. Some grieving parents attempt to channel their anger into something that will help others. One example is the case of Amber Hagerman. She was nine years old when she was abducted while riding her bike in January of 1996. Her body was found four days later, and her killer was never caught. Her parents became advocates for tougher laws to protect children from predators. As a result, the Amber Alert System was born. This system would go on to save hundreds of lives, as it alerts the media when a person under eighteen goes missing and may be in danger. This is an example of doing something good in the face of tragedy. Amber's legacy will continue to save lives nationally and even abroad, as it is implemented in all fifty states and even internationally. [2]

Bargaining. The next stage that Kübler-Ross identified was the bargaining stage. This stage is often seen in cases of terminal illness, in which the dying person or his or her loved ones bargain, or negotiate, for a different outcome. Often this bargaining is with God or a higher power of some sort. Some people make promises, such as "If you only save her, I will be a better person," or "I will give to charity."

Depression. When it becomes clear the difficult event did, in fact, occur, depression can set in. This can cause despair along with such thoughts as, "What is the point? I just don't care anymore." People can experience depression in which both the physical and

Denial is a common response to loss. The first moments after waking up each morning may hold the surprise that your spouse is not beside you. It becomes a survivor's task to accept the loss and to eventually adjust to his or her new existence.

emotional aspects of their lives can be altered, such as having feelings of immense sadness along with disturbances in sleep patterns, eating habits, and concentration.

People who are feeling depressed may feel sad, fatigued, show a loss of interest in things, have changes in sleep or weight, and may feel hopeless and even suicidal. It is important for loved ones and friends to be aware of situations in which someone's sadness about the death of a loved one turns into depression. The person may be in need of professional help.

Acceptance. Reaching this stage does not mean that one is necessarily happy. Once it becomes clear that this new reality has emerged, people understand that they cannot change this situation and must learn to cope with it in the best way possible. For those who have lost a loved one, this is the time when denial is no longer present and the stark reality emerges—that life will have to go on without this loved one.

Not every person goes through each stage in this order. Some stages may overlap or be skipped altogether. But Kübler-Ross's stages of grief theory does give some insight into the emotional turmoil that a person grieving experiences in the aftermath of an event.

Expanding Grief Research

Two psychiatrists wanting to improve upon Kübler-Ross's ideas of a grief process, John Bowlby and Colin Murray Parkes, created their own four-phase model of grief. It focuses on the attachments people have with others in their life. Some of the emotions in their stages overlap with the ideas of Kübler-Ross's model.

Numbness. In the first phase, people who experience a loss are shocked and numb. They understand what has happened, but it has not become a reality to them. They are in a state of disbelief. They may make decisions, arrange for the funeral, and talk to loved ones, but all the while they are feeling as if they are in a daze or a dream state. It is the mind's way of protecting itself against reality. The reality will hit them in time, but right now, they are protecting themselves. This allows the person to still be able to function in the worst circumstances.

Yearning. In the second phase, the reality has started to sink in. Here people struggle with intense emotions. They may experience anger and guilt and think of all the possible if onlys, but mostly they just long for the person who has died. They may see their loved one in their dreams and think they hear his or her voice. They want more than anything to turn back time, make this situation right, and stop feeling this overwhelming grief and pain. They cannot visualize a world without the person who is now gone.

Disorganization and despair. In the third phase, it becomes clear that the deceased person is not coming back. As a result, the people grieving may feel despair, depression, and apathy toward life. They may have a hard time returning to everyday life and, as a result, have a hard time managing responsibilities in their lives.

Reorganization. When grieving people reach this stage, they have accepted the loss. Their life may never be the same, but they are able to go on living. The intense feelings of grief will occur less frequently, and the apathy they were feeling toward life will subside. In this phase, grieving people will make an effort to connect with those who are still living.

Completion of Tasks

J. William Worden, who took issue with grief stages, claims that while adapting to their new life without their loved one, people must complete a set of tasks in order to complete mourning.[3] The completion of these tasks does not necessarily have to be done in this order.

Task I: To accept the reality of the loss. As mentioned in Parkes and Bowlby's research, there is a sense of disbelief when someone has died. In this task, grieving people must accept the fact that their loved one is gone and is not coming back. Here they may experience dreams of the deceased person or may even think they catch a glimpse of him or her in a restaurant or on a bus. To work

Looking at photographs and reliving memories are positive ways for children to remember the deceased.

through this task, grieving people must get through any denial and understand that their loved one is gone.

Task II: To work through the pain of the grief. Grieving people need to face the feelings associated with grief. These may be feelings of sadness, anger, anxiety, guilt, or loneliness. Whatever the feelings are, they should not be suppressed or avoided because they may show up later on in life if they are not worked through.[4] Many grieving people are just not prepared to face the intensity of the emotions that occur during grief, and it can be a natural response to try to avoid them.

Task III: To adjust to an environment in which the deceased is missing. Worden speaks of three types of adjustments that people need to make after they have lost a loved one: external, internal, and spiritual. External adjustments include getting used to everyday life without the deceased person. Internal adjustments describe how grieving people feel now that their loved one is gone. During this adjustment, there is a focus on how the loss has affected their sense of self. Lastly, spiritual adjustments include how the grieving person now sees the world and their belief system.

Task IV: To emotionally relocate the deceased and move on with life. This task may prove to be the most difficult for people who are grieving.[5] Here, grieving people need to allow themselves to love again. Their life cannot stop when their loved one dies. They need to go on. They need to live with the memories of that person, but they need to live, nonetheless.

Worden differentiates his list of tasks from stages, pointing out that in his model, each task can be revisited and reworked over time. People can go through them differently and at different times. This allows people to feel that they can grieve at their own pace and in their own way.

When Grief Is Complicated

Some researchers have been taking a new approach to grief. Focusing on companionship rather than treatment, Alan D. Wolfelt,

Ph.D., addresses the importance of being emotionally available for a person in mourning. In his book *Understanding Grief: Helping Yourself Heal,* he discusses how it is more helpful to be there as support for a person rather than being there to treat the person. He also distinguishes normal grief from complicated grief. Complicated grief issues include:

Postponing grief: Delaying expression of grief indefinitely

Displacing grief: Directing feelings of grief to other parts of one's life

Replacing grief: Investing feelings in another relationship in an effort to avoid grieving

Minimizing grief: Using rationalization to minimize feelings of grief

Somatizing grief: Converting feelings of grief into physical symptoms[6]

Each of these, according to Wolfelt, is a way for people to avoid the feelings associated with grief and can be a sign of complicated grief, which may require the help of a professional grief therapist.

New Grief Research

A study from the *Journal of the American Academy of Child and Adolescent Psychiatry* analyzed children and their risk for prolonged grief reactions. These reactions would be similar to the complicated grief symptoms discussed earlier. Children with these types of reactions could be at risk for depression. The study looked at 182 children and teens between eight and seventeen years of age who had suddenly lost a parent. They were assessed at nine, twenty-one and thirty-three months after their parent died.

The researchers found that in more than half of the participants, the grief reactions had significantly decreased by the twenty-one-month mark. However, 10 percent of the participants did show prolonged grief reactions that lasted almost three years. This put those children at risk for depression and functional impairment in their lives. This type of research is important because it gives mental health and medical professionals information that will help them to identify children and teens who are at risk for mental health issues due to the sudden loss of a parent. These types of studies are helpful in giving the researchers a good look at the participants over a span of time. They can then analyze the results and see patterns of behavior. This is especially useful when studying grief in children and teens, as this will give an indication of what their needs might be and how family, friends, and professionals can best provide support to them.[7]

Age Can Impact Responses

Researchers are conflicted about the ways in which children mourn. Can infants mourn the loss of a parent if they cannot comprehend death? This question is often debated by grief experts in the field, and no true consensus has been reached. However, most would agree that children have to have a mental image of the loved one and must also be aware of their constant presence in their life to really mourn that person.[8] This level of understanding is usually present around three to four years of age.[9]

Worden, who developed the tasks associated with grief, states that children's emotional, cognitive, and social development must be considered when looking at a child's mourning process. He holds that his task theory can be applied to children, but depending on their level of understanding, they may have difficulty with some of the tasks. If a child is not able to understand finality, he or she may have a hard time with the first task of accepting the reality of the loss.[10]

Developmental level has an effect on a child's ability to understand loss. Some children display what is known as magical thinking—a type of nonscientific reasoning that includes such ideas as connections between unrelated events and the mind's ability to affect the physical world. For instance, children may believe that somehow they have caused the death and feel guilty as a result. Some children are worried that they will die soon, too. The emotions that affect children are more complicated because of their level of understanding of death and their surroundings in general. They may not be able to fully comprehend the loss and, as a result, may not experience many of the emotions of grief that an adult might.

Researchers may disagree with each other regarding which emotion is felt most strongly during the grieving process and how adults and children handle grief. However, the psychiatric community agrees on one thing—grieving people are going to go through an array of emotions, and those emotions will affect them for a long time.

The Loss of Someone Close

A child's family of origin is so important in how they view their environment and the world. Family includes parents, siblings, grandparents, aunts, uncles, cousins, and in some cases guardians even if they are not biological relatives. When a young person experiences the loss of a family member, it can have a drastic impact. Also, the type of relationship the child had with the person impacts the grief process.

Losing a parent can create emotions in a child that they might not experience with the loss of a sibling or cousin. A child comes into this world completely dependent on his or her parents for everything—food, shelter, and love. Children often think the world of their parents. For many children, no person on earth can match their mom or dad. For many parents, the love for a child is unconditional. Parents will love their children regardless of how they look or behave.

When children lose a parent, it can feel as if the world as they know it has come crashing down upon them. The familiar place they may have known as home has disappeared, and what is left is sadness and uncertainty—uncertainty about what will happen now and who will take care of them. Even after the initial shock and sorrow subside, there will be difficult days ahead. Children soon realize that for those milestones of life—birthdays, graduations, weddings— their parent will not be there. These joyous occasions will never be entirely happy, as there will always be a missing piece—the parent who has died. Children can often wonder, "Why me?" They may question why this tragedy has happened to them and may feel that life is not fair.

A Newly Single Parent

When a parent dies, often the surviving parent is left to keep everything together. He or she is grieving, too, but there are still responsibilities. The surviving parent may mourn when it is quiet and no one else is around. He or she may be lonely and have anxiety about the future. The parent who is left or the guardian who is now tasked with caring for young children must take on this two-person job alone. Grieving while caring for a family and home can be a challenge. A household that may have had two people contributing to it now only has one.

The shift in the household responsibilities can create additional anxieties for the parent or guardian and the children. The family will need to work as a team to try to deal with their new family dynamic. Issues can arise with this new dynamic in the household that are unfamiliar to the family. The surviving parent may begin to worry about his or her own mortality. The children may worry about this, as well. There is a great deal of responsibility that now falls onto the surviving spouse, so the person may feel responsible for improving his or her health as a way to cope with these feelings. The children may also encourage the parent to try to get healthier or to stop bad habits, such as eating junk food, as poor eating could cause health problems in the future.

The surviving parent is also working through their own grief during a time that they need to be able to help their children work through their emotions. This can be a difficult challenge for the parent. In trying to stay strong, the surviving parent may unknowingly be sending a message to the children that they are over their grief, and the children may feel pressure to get over their grief, as well.[1] Communication is important during this time. It is a good idea for the parent to get education from professionals in the field about what to look for in their grieving child to best be able to help them through this process. Children are not as mature as adults, and they do not have the same cognitive abilities as adults.[2] This means that a child or teen's grief process can look different than what adults are expecting in a situation like this. Factors that impact this can be the age of the child or teen, their developmental level, and any special needs they may have.

Some parents decide after time has elapsed that they want a new partner to share their life with. Many people remarry after their spouse has died. If there are children involved, even adult children, this can sometimes cause turmoil within the family. It can be further complicated if the new partner also has children because the families may now merge and live together.

Blended Families

Acquiring a stepfamily can be a stressful process. Children have not chosen this family. In some cases, they have not even been consulted in this decision. In their mind, the situation may feel forced. There may be feelings that the surviving parent is betraying the memory of the deceased parent. If children accept this new person, they may feel as if they are betraying the deceased parent. This is not an uncommon reaction for young children, teens, and even adult children in this type of situation. Children who have lost a parent usually do not want someone to replace that parent. There is usually

When one parent dies, the surviving parent may turn to an unhealthy lifestyle for comfort, which can cause their children to become overly concerned about the remaining parent's health.

a special place for that parent that can never be filled, and if the child feels that someone is trying to take the dead parent's place, conflict can arise.

It can be helpful for parents to discuss the issue of remarriage or moving in together before it actually happens to give children time to let this information sink in and ensure they do not feel blindsided.

Providing Support

Since the bond between a parent and child is so strong, when a teen loses a parent, everyone left in the family needs to look out for that teen and provide emotional support. One goal might be to provide support so teens do not have to look for unhealthy ways to deal with their feelings, such as drugs or alcohol. There is enough confusion in the teenage years without a major loss. Add to it the death of a parent, and this could be the mixture for self-destruction. Even though other family members are dealing with their own grief, they need to look out for teens during this time.

It is important for surviving parents to try to keep things as normal as possible. If Friday night is movie night, for instance, that tradition should be continued. Teens may feel guilty about continuing with movie night when one parent has died. They may feel guilty for having fun and may believe that the deceased parent would think that he or she is not missed. But teens need to understand that most parents would want them to be happy and not to mourn indefinitely. It is important that teens realize it is okay to go on with life and enjoy themselves again.

Everyone needs to feel that the way he or she has chosen to grieve is okay because each person grieves in his or her own unique way. Some children feel they want to talk about the deceased parent. For others, it is too painful, and they choose not to speak of the person, at least not right away. Any way that they are coping, so long as it is not destructive or harmful to themselves or others, should be respected.

Encountering the first holiday or birthday following a loved one's death can be painful and confusing. Aside from missing the lost friend or relative, survivors can feel guilty celebrating.

Sometimes children worry that they will forget the parent who has died. Unlike the surviving parent, the child may not have had as many years with that person, and memories may fade. If a child wants to talk about the deceased parent, this should be fostered by the rest of the family, as talking about that person will keep the memories alive for the child.

Lifelong Impact of Loss

A study was conducted to examine the factors that contribute to mental health issues in adulthood in those who suffered the loss of a parent. The study, from the journal *Psychological Trauma: Theory, Research, Practice and Policy,* examined data collected from the National Comorbidity Survey-Replication, and they looked at things such as the age of the person when they lost their parent, how long it had been since they lost their parent, and if they suffered neglect or harm at the hands of the parent.[3]

The researchers then looked at lifetime mental disorders, such as mood disorders, anxiety disorders, substance abuse disorders, eating disorders, and intermittent explosive disorder. They thought they would see poorer mental health associated with certain factors, such as the death of a parent at a younger age, the death of the parent at a more recent time, and adverse or neglectful parenting practices. What they found was the loss of a parent earlier in life was consistent with most anxiety and mood disorders, substance use, and intermittent explosive disorder. They also found that the younger the person was when the parent died, the more consistent this was with mental health issues in adulthood. This study, although looking at the age of the person who lost their parent, did not focus only on childhood as some previous research had. Rather, it focused on this loss over the lifespan, and the results supported the connection between the age of the loss of a parent and issues in adulthood. Since the relationship between parent and child transforms as the child matures and becomes an adult, it is important to study parental loss across the developmental lifespan.

Confusing Emotions

Anger toward the parent who has died is not uncommon. Children can feel abandoned, then they may feel guilty for being angry at the deceased parent—this cycle can continue on and on. It can help for children who lose a parent to talk to other children or teens going through the same thing. This way, they will know that some emotions are common among children left behind. They will be able to feel that they truly are talking to another person who understands what they are going through, and he or she may find peace in that.

The surviving parent is suffering the loss of his or her spouse, though it is different from losing a parent. Being there for each other is important, but just as the surviving parent can benefit from talking about his or her emotions with other people who have lost a spouse, children who have lost a parent can be helped by talking to other children in the same situation.

Every year, things will come up that stir up emotions—Mother's Day or Father's Day, birthdays, holidays, or the anniversary of the parent's death. Having a support system in place can help children and teens get through these emotional times. Friends of the grieving teen may never have experienced loss. They are fortunate in this regard. However, this can create a situation where the grieving teen feels misunderstood and may have trouble talking about some of their bad days because they feel their friends don't understand. Creating a support system of people who have been in similar situations can help with the grieving process.

4

Changing Family Dynamic

Siblings are an important part of a young person's life. Whether they fight, get along, or both, the relationship between siblings in the home is an important part of the family dynamic. When a teen loses their brother or sister, it can help for that person to share his or her feelings. Sometimes, however, the person doesn't know with whom they should share these feelings. Not only is the teen suffering the loss of a brother or sister, he or she must also see the grief that other family members are going through during this time. Younger siblings may not fully comprehend the situation. Often young children do not understand that death means the person is never coming back. They lack the ability to understand the finality of it. The parents who lost their child are experiencing an immense amount of pain. They have to console their surviving children while also dealing with their own grief. This creates a situation where the older child or teen may feel the need to take care of their younger siblings and also to be strong for their parents. This can put undue stress on the grieving teen.

People do not expect that they will bury their children. It goes against the natural order of things. So when people lose a child, it might be the single most devastating experience of their life. Parents who have suffered this loss may be in a state of shock and complete disbelief. When the shock subsides, intense sadness and grief can occur. Each member of the family is grieving in his or her own way. They are all trying to be there for other remaining family members while also dealing with the intense grief that they are suffering. The family unit, at this point, is in crisis.

The New Normal

The surviving siblings may feel awkward leaning on their parents for support when they see that their parents are in so much pain. Teens in crisis may then choose to bottle up their emotions because they don't want to further upset the already grieving parents and younger siblings. The family is a unit—a compilation of unique pieces— where each member has his or her own place in the unit. After the death of a child, that unit is disrupted and may feel incomplete. The unit that the family had come to know does not exist and will never exist again because a piece of the puzzle is gone forever. A new family unit will emerge without the deceased sibling, and each person in the family must learn to function in this new unit. Families may not know how to function at first. They may need counseling as a family, as well as individual counseling for each member of the family. To try to pretend that nothing has happened and go on with life as if nothing has changed can be harmful, especially to the surviving siblings, who may not fully understand what has occurred.

Marital Stress

The grief over the loss of a child is so strong that many marriages are not able to survive this crisis. Sometimes one spouse does not understand the coping mechanisms of the other spouse. One spouse might blame the other for the child's death or might have his or her own feelings of guilt. Sometimes anxiety or depression gets to be too much for the relationship to withstand.

When a child dies, one spouse may like to talk about that child. She may feel that this is keeping the child's memory alive, which may be helping her with the healing process. The other spouse, however, may not be ready for this and may find it too painful to talk about the child. Neither spouse may understand the other's grieving process. "How can she want to talk about him all day and dig up all of these horrible feelings?" one might think. The other spouse may ask, "How can he just forget about him so quickly?" Each person is

The loss of a child puts an enormous amount of stress on the child's parents. Couples may handle their grief differently. Many marriages are unable to survive such stress.

devastated, but each is dealing with grief in his or her own unique way. Sometimes the inability to understand and communicate with each other about this grief can cause the marriage to fail.

Regrets

In most households, siblings are a constant presence in each other's lives, whether they get along or are constantly bickering. For children and teens, losing a sibling may mean that they feel uncertain about their own place in the family unit. The loss of the constant presence of their sibling is an adjustment that often proves difficult for those

The loss of a sibling brings up not only sadness but also guilt. Many siblings irrationally blame themselves for fighting with their brother or sister when they were alive.

children left behind. Many young people who have lost siblings deal with feelings of guilt and regret.

Guilt is a big part of dealing with the death of a sibling. Brothers and sisters commonly bicker and fight. It is natural. When people live together, there are bound to be arguments—even more so if the people are siblings. Sometimes, siblings may think about how wonderful it would be to be an only child and doted on by both parents. Such wishes are usually fleeting and nothing more than an emotional response to a dispute with a sibling. When people lose a brother or sister and they think back to unkind thoughts they had or mean words they said, they may feel a tremendous amount of guilt. This feeling is normal, but sibling rivalry is normal, too.

It is important not to get caught up in a cycle of self-blame for arguing with the deceased sibling. Since members of the immediate family are grieving much like the teen is, it may be helpful to talk to a pastor, a counselor, an aunt or uncle, or another member of the extended family. Teens can begin to work through these feelings of guilt by talking about what they wish they had said or done when their sibling was still alive.[1] It is important for those working with children and teens who are grieving the loss of a sibling to understand that these feelings of guilt are very real. Some surviving siblings actually feel a sense of guilt about the death itself—that in some way they caused it either by their actions or angry thoughts.[2] This is a tremendous burden to carry, and it is one that may impede further emotional growth if not worked through. If the surviving sibling's actions did contribute to the death in some way, then professional help would be a likely course due to the complex nature of the emotions involved in this type of situation.

Research in the area of the loss of a sibling has found that this type of loss can impact a teen later in life. An article entitled "Complicated Grief and Bereavement in Young Adults Following Close Friend and Sibling Loss" described a study that examined the connection between different types of loss and the quality of the relationship with complicated grief, depression, physical symptoms, and assumptions about the world.[3] The assumptions analyzed included how the grieving person saw meaningfulness and benevolence in the world around them and their feelings of self-worth. The type of relationship that was explored were those who lost a sibling or a close friend and the quality of relationship was examined. Whether the two were close and whether there was conflict was examined in the results, as well.

The researchers conducted the study with 107 young adults between the ages of seventeen and twenty-nine. These participants fell into two groups: those were had experienced loss and those who had not. The findings of the study showed that those who had lost a sibling showed a greater depth in their relationship than those who had lost a friend. Also, they found that 19 percent of young adults who suffered a loss met the criteria for complicated grief and 37 percent suffered from mild to severe depression. The participants who lost a sibling were more likely to have complicated grief, and they reported more symptoms of complicated grief compared to those who lost a close friend. This demonstrates how the loss of a sibling is difficult for young people due to the closeness of the relationship and how this loss can impact the surviving sibling later in life.

First Grief Experience

For many teens, the loss of their grandparent will be the first experience they have with death. A study entitled "Death Anxiety and Personal Growth in Adolescents Experiencing the Death of a Grandparent" looked at this particular type of loss and its relation to death anxiety or a fear of the dying process.[1] The researchers in this study wanted to look at adolescents in particular due to the fact that they are undergoing a unique developmental process. They explored the relationship between the grandchild and grandparent while studying 226 respondents. The respondents were between the ages of eleven and eighteen, and they completed a questionnaire as part of the study. Of the respondents, 124 had already experienced the loss of a grandparent. This meant that more than half of those participating in the study had already experienced this loss before becoming an adult.

Relationship With Grandparents

Grandparents often find a new youthfulness when a grandchild is welcomed into the family. They get to enjoy their grandchildren without stressing over parental issues.

Grandparents have raised their children, and now their children have children. Their only job is to love their grandchildren. They get to play with them and have fun. They can just sit and watch these children grow up. Many feel they have earned this privilege, and they relish it.

A grandparent's home may be the one place where a child feels truly loved without judgment. Teens especially have conflicts of opinion with parents. The adolescent years can create some distance between parents and their teens, as young people are often trying to figure out life and gain independence. However, these issues may not overlap into a teen's relationship with a grandparent, so this may feel like a safe and loving relationship for the adolescent.

Grandparent as the Parent

Some children are raised by their grandparents. A grandparent may become the temporary guardian of children or teens if their mother or father is having difficulty managing the responsibilities of raising children along with the other stressors of life, such as work and paying bills. In other cases, the grandparent becomes the permanent guardian for his or her grandchildren. This could happen as a result of the death of a parent or abandonment by a parent. In this scenario, the grandparent is the parental figure and has the same duties of all other parents, including becoming the disciplinarian.

The United States Census Bureau found that in 2010, 2.7 million grandparents were responsible for the basic needs of one or more grandchildren under eighteen who was living with them. Grandmothers made up 1.7 million of this number, and 1 million were grandfathers. Overall, in that year, the agency found that 5.4 million children under eighteen were living in a grandparent's home. [2] Therefore, it is important to look closely at this relationship

The loss of a grandparent can be devastating, particularly if the grandparent acted as a primary caregiver. When a parent cannot take care of his or her children, a grandparent often steps in.

between the grandchild and grandparent, as so many young people live in the same household as their grandparent.

When a grandparent is raising a child or teenager, the two frequently forge a close relationship. The grandparent can be seen as a parental figure and a fun person to spend time with. However, when a grandparent steps into the role of guardian for the adolescent, there may be some friction because often teenagers are developing their own identity and may be rebellious. Now the fun-loving grandparent is put into the role of the enforcer, and the dynamic may shift. As a result, the relationship between grandparent and grandchild can become strained.

When Grandparents Die

As the earlier research stated, the death of a grandparent can be the first major loss a teen ever suffers. It may be sudden, following an event such as a heart attack, or it may be gradual and take place after years of illness. When a grandparent dies suddenly and unexpectedly, grandchildren may go through periods of disbelief and denial. In other situations, grandchildren must learn to cope with the loss of a grandparent well before the grandparent dies, as in the case of long-term debilitating illnesses. It is important to distinguish between these types of losses, as a lengthy illness can create stress and stir emotions that are unique to that situation.

Illness and Grief

Unfortunately, many older adults experience a decrease in their cognitive abilities as they progress through the years.[3] Older adults can experience memory problems, a decrease in the ability to recall information, and a decrease in the ability to process information. A grandparent may be experiencing some of these problems merely as the result of aging. However, for some grandparents, these can be signs of a more serious health condition.

One such condition is Alzheimer's disease, a serious brain disorder. More than five millions American age sixty-five and older currently have Alzheimer's disease.[4] It is the most common type of dementia, or the loss of mental functions to a degree severe enough to interfere with daily functioning. With Alzheimer's disease, nerve cells in the brain die, and the signals that need to be transmitted through the brain for a person to function have difficulty completing transmission. As a result, memory, judgment, and thinking can become impaired. The decline in cognitive abilities of a grandparent may go unnoticed for a long time. Sometimes it is difficult for family members to discern when memory and thinking problems are just a part of aging and when they may indicate a serious condition, such as Alzheimer's. It can, however, progress to the point where the grandparent is not able to recognize his or her own grandchild.

The debilitating nature of Alzheimer's disease and other physical and mental ailments that affect the elderly, such as cancer, heart disease, and stroke, can take years to develop. For families, it is often difficult to watch a loved one's mind and body deteriorate. This can be especially hard for teens. Often, teens may feel as though they have lost a grandparent long before the grandparent actually dies. With illnesses that affect cognition, it can feel as if the family no longer knows this person and that the person no longer knows his or her family members. With cancer and other debilitating diseases that attack the body, the grandparent may now look totally different. Sometimes people dying of an illness become depressed or moody. This is not a reflection of their feelings toward their grandchildren. They are grieving, too. They may know that the outlook is bleak. They may realize that they only have a short time left and are grieving the time with their family they will never have. Good days and bad days should be expected, and bad days should not be taken personally. The entire family is in a state of crisis when a loved one is dying.

People can experience the grieving process well before the actual death of a loved one. They may be in denial that it is really happening. They may feel anger about the situation and the fact that

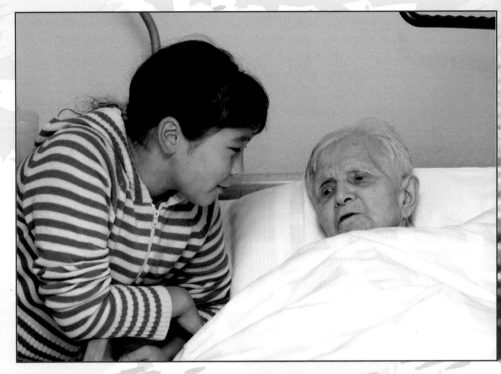

When a grandparent suffers from dementia and certain illnesses, it can feel as if loved ones have lost them already. It is difficult to accept when a grandparent no longer recognizes you.

they can not change it. They may yearn for a time when the dying person was healthy.

Many people are uncomfortable around someone who is very ill and may distance themselves from the pain. It is hard for people to watch someone they love suffer. It is important to have a sounding board—someone to discuss feelings with. There are support groups just for grandchildren mourning the loss of a grandparent. Sometimes it helps to be with people who are going through a similar experience.

Dementia can stem from causes other than Alzheimer's disease. It can create a situation where the person with dementia is doing things or treating their loved ones in ways they never have before.

This can be difficult not just for the teen but also the entire family, and it can put stress on a person and impact their ability to deal with their grief.

A study in the journal *Clinical Gerontologist* looked at eighty participants in the Midwestern region of the United States who were caregivers providing for people with mild, moderate, or severe dementia.[5] The researchers looked at anticipatory grief, which is grief that happens when a person is anticipating the loss of a loved one. The researchers looked at different factors, including the behavior of the person with dementia and also the duties the caretaker undertook when providing for their loved one. Caretakers were asked about behavioral changes in their loved one, which could include disruptive behavior, memory changes, and sadness. The researchers found that the frequency of behavioral changes was the best predicator for anticipatory grief. Things such as long hours of caregiving and physical impairments of the loved one were not as good of an indicator for anticipatory grief. The research found that it was not the stress of caregiving duties that impacted anticipatory grief of caretakers but rather the change in behavior they saw in their loved one. Given this research, caregivers may want to join a support group given the difficulties associated with taking care of a loved one with dementia.

Automobile accidents are an all-too-common cause of teen fatalities. Teen drivers are at risk because they are inexperienced, and their ability to make sound judgements is not fully developed.

Death of a Young Person

It is difficult for people to make sense of a young person's death. When a grandparent dies, as has been covered in the previous chapter, often the death is seen as more natural due to the fact that the grandparent is older than the others in the family. Maybe they lived a long and happy life, so it is sad but ultimately the people who love the person know they lived their life to the fullest. However, when a young person dies, it is often called unnatural and tragic. A young person's death could be due to a health condition, such as a heart defect or cancer, a drug overdose, a murder, suicide, an accident, or a myriad of other reasons. However, in all of those cases, it can still feel unfair to the friends and family left behind that this person's life was cut short. Grief responses of teens to the death of a young person can be complicated by the circumstances surrounding the death. Was it a suicide? Did they put their own life at risk somehow? Did the person suffer during the last period of their life from a disease, such as cancer? All of these facts can impact the way a teen works through their grief when mourning the loss of a young person.

Accidental Deaths

Motor vehicle accidents are the leading cause of death for twelve- to nineteen-year-olds in the United States.[1] Teens are less likely to wear seat belts when compared to adults, which contributes to the high fatality rate of teens involved in car accidents.[2] Many of these accidents are alcohol-related. In addition, some are due to the young driver being distracted or inexperienced. Many teen automobile deaths occur during prom and graduation celebrations from April through June.[3]

According to these high statistics, many teens will experience the sudden and traumatic loss of a friend while in high school or college. Because friends and social groups are so important during the teenage years, this sudden loss can prove devastating for those friends left behind. Often teens do not know where to turn for help in dealing with these emotions. If it was an alcohol-related event, teens may feel angry at the friend who was killed or even angry at themselves, as they figure they could have done something to stop their friend from driving or getting into a car with someone who had been drinking.

Substance Abuse

Drug use is another killer of teens in the United States. During the teen years, curiosity can peak. Unfortunately, for some this means experimenting with drugs and alcohol. Teenagers do not always understand the risks associated with drug and alcohol use. A teen may experiment with these things to satisfy curiosity, fit in, socialize, combat boredom, relax, or relieve the pressures of life. Those at risk for drug and alcohol abuse include teens with a family history of drug and alcohol abuse, teens who are depressed or have low self-esteem, teens who feel like outcasts among their peers, and teens going through a traumatic event. Two things to look for that may indicate a teen is abusing drugs or alcohol are as follows.

Emotional changes. Sudden mood swings, personality changes, paranoia, self-destructive behavior, irritability, demands for privacy, changes in appearance, worsening grades, giddy behavior, changes in friends, depression, apathy toward things once important to the teen, and poor decision making.

Physical changes. Red and glazed eyes with changes in pupil size, changes in appetite, changes in sleep patterns, poor coordination, shaky hands, blank stare, cough or runny nose, nausea, vomiting, sweating, smell of substance on person and clothes, needle marks, puffiness or paleness of the face, or hyperactivity.

Any of these can be an indication that something is wrong. It is important to be aware of these signs so that teens can notice a peer who may be in trouble. Many drug overdoses in teens are accidental and could have been avoided. That is why it is so important for teens to look out for each other. If someone suspects a friend to be abusing drugs and alcohol, it is important to talk to the friend and encourage him or her to get help. There are treatment facilities that specialize in helping teens. If the person denies that he or she has a problem, it might help to talk with a counselor who specializes in helping teens in order to get information and tips on how to approach this person

School Shootings

In recent years, there have been multiple mass shootings that have taken place in school settings.

In these situations, students experience an especially difficult loss. Some may have been wounded in the attack. Others were not hurt but witnessed the violence and have to deal with that trauma, as well. Most are mourning not one friend or teacher but several. School violence of this type can take a heavy toll on communities.

again about drug or alcohol abuse. Encouraging the teen to contact a professional may help get him or her on the road to recovery.

Bullying and Suicide

Not all drug-related deaths among teens are accidental. Some young people decide to take their own life. Suicide is the third leading cause of death for twelve- to nineteen-year-olds.[4] This is a problem that needs to be addressed in the community, in schools, and in the home. It is important for parents, school personnel, and friends to know what signs to look for if they are concerned that a teen may be depressed or struggling to cope with the stressors of life. In 2010, more than half of the suicides in the United States were done with a gun.[5] Therefore, it is important for parents to make sure guns are not accessible to teens in the home.

Girls differ from boys when it comes to suicide. Data have indicated that girls think about suicide more than boys do and even attempt it twice as often as boys do by using drugs or cutting themselves. However, a boy is four times more likely to die as a result of suicide because boys tend to use more lethal methods, such as guns or hanging.[6] Any time teens express a desire to take their own life, it should be taken seriously. It could be a cry for help that is asking for someone to intervene during this difficult time. No discussion of suicide should ever be taken lightly. It helps to be educated in what to look out for, as this will help people be able to identify behaviors in friends that might put them at risk.

Today bullying is a big problem in schools and communities across the country. In some cases, bullying is so bad for a teen or young person that they feel hopeless and may attempt suicide. Bullying has changed over the years. Before the Internet and social media, if a teen were bullied, it happened at school or in the community, but the person could at least try to get a reprieve while at home. Now, with twenty-four-hour access to email, texting, and social media, teens are subjected to constant bullying that comes in many forms across many different platforms. Cyberbullying is

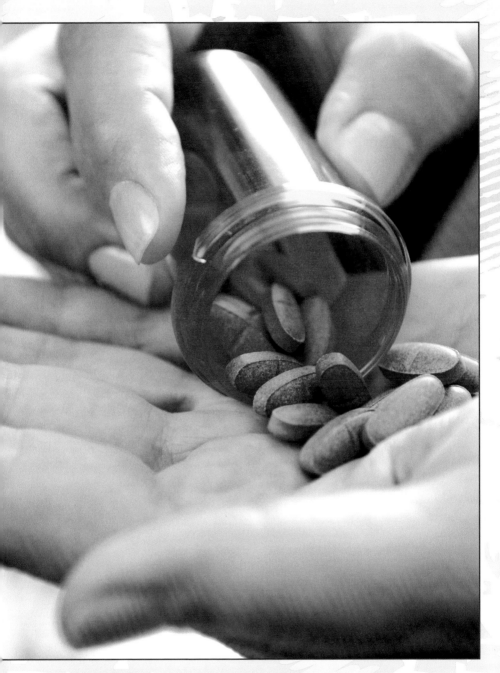

Girls are more likely to attempt suicide than are boys. But girls tend to use methods such as overdosing on pills and wrist-slashing, which have a higher chance of survival than guns and other deadlier means.

the name for this type of bullying. It happens on social media, via text message and email, and through various online platforms and applications. It goes on outside of school, and it can be relentless.

On January 14, 2010, fifteen-year-old Phoebe Prince of Massachusetts hung herself.[7] Over a three-month span, Phoebe was verbally abused by classmates both in public and on social media. On the day of her death, her bullies continued the harassment and even told Phoebe to kill herself. She did. Some criminal charges followed, and the nation took notice of this problem plaguing young people in society. School districts across the country are now making an effort to combat bullying in school so no teen ever feels that suicide is the way out. Educating students, teachers, and administrators about bullying, its impact, and the ways to prevent it and deal with it when it does happen is imperative in stopping bullying in schools.

Seeking Help

One way to begin to help a friend in need is to talk to him or her. Many teens just want to be heard. Just letting a friend talk while listening without judgment may help him or her gather the strength to get through a difficult time. Be sure to tell an adult or a mental health professional in order to get help immediately if a friend says that he or she wants to die or is thinking of suicide. When a person confides suicidal feelings in a friend, he or she is often calling out for help.

Not all teens will ask for help, nor will they give any indication that they are suicidal. Sometimes a suicide comes as a complete shock. The family and friends of this person may then feel guilty and think that they missed something. They might blame themselves and think that had they only been more observant, this would not have happened. Sometimes a person is determined to take his or her own life, and there is nothing anyone can do to change that.

The death of a friend by suicide is extremely difficult to cope with because in addition to the loss of a friend, there may be issues of anger and resentment toward the person who took his or her own life. The grieving family members and friends of a suicide victim may move through the different emotions of grief that most grieving people deal with; however, when a loved one has chosen to take his or her own life, this comes as a traumatic shock. To compound this issue, the grieving people may feel as though they are being judged by others and may feel lonely and isolated.

Teens going through this loss may have a difficult time comprehending why their loved one has chosen to take this path and why he or she did not think about others when making this decision. Teens may be angry because they feel that the suicide was a way of getting back at them or hurting them for some reason. All of these emotions are normal reactions to such a traumatic event. That is why it is important for those grieving a loved one who has committed suicide to get support from peers in a similar situation. The anger and guilt can become overwhelming, especially for teens. Parents and family members of grieving teens need to be there for them, listen, and offer support. This is a difficult time, and they need the love and support of family members and friends now more than ever.

Pets Are Family Too

Experiencing the loss of a pet is something many people can relate to in their lives. The shorter lives of pets in comparison to human beings means that people generally outlive their pets. For many, their pet is their friend, their family, and a big part of their life. The loss of a pet may be the first loss a child or teen experiences. As discussed in previous chapters, grief occurs when a person suffers a loss. The grief a teen feels when their pet has died is real. There may be people in the life of the teen who downplay this loss, but for the teen, this can feel like they have lost their best friend. Understanding that the teen may need support while dealing with this grief is important.

For many people, their relationship with their pet may have all of the attributes of a great friendship without the conflicts that exist in human relationships. Pets offer companionship without judgment. To a pet owner, this animal may represent the purest of relationships. To have this relationship cut short can be painful. As a result, the pet owner may have some of the same emotions and reactions discussed in earlier chapters because he or she has, in fact, lost a loved one. Lack of concentration, disbelief, and extreme sadness can all be part of the process of grieving a pet.

Oprah Winfrey made news in the summer of 2007 when Gracie, her two-year-old golden retriever, died suddenly. On May 26, 2007, Winfrey received news from one of her dog walkers that Gracie had choked on a plastic ball. Winfrey was shocked and devastated by the loss of her beloved animal. In her magazine, she remembered the upsetting event:

> Gone??!! I couldn't believe what I was hearing. Yes, I saw it. I saw the caretaker rocking back and forth on the ground, his arms wrapped around himself, crying hysterically. My brain took in the whole scene, but it wasn't tracking properly. The first thing I remember saying is, "It's okay. It'll be okay. Tell me what happened." Through his sobs I heard: ". . . choked on a ball." And I knew, this was real. Gracie is gone, Gracie is gone, Gracie is gone kept repeating in my head.[1]

Through Gracie's death, Winfrey says, she received a message, as if she should take something away from this sad event. The message was, "Slow down, you're moving too fast."[2]

Pet Loss

Pet loss can come in many different forms. The pet can die peacefully in its sleep from old age or die in an accident like Winfrey's Gracie. The circumstances may be different in these scenarios, but the outcome is the same. The pet is gone, and the grieving process begins. In some cases, the pet might have run away. Other times, a family has to return the pet or give it away because it is just not working out. Maybe the family needs to move and the new apartment or home does not allow pets. Maybe they are military family and they have orders to move overseas. Whatever the circumstances, there is a sense of loss that may stir up many different emotions.

Guilt can be a big part of the grieving process for a pet. If a pet is suffering and has a poor quality of life, the pet owner has the option of euthanizing the pet, or having it put to sleep by a veterinarian. Many pet owners do not make this decision lightly. Usually they have a number of conversations with a veterinarian about the pet's quality of life and the prognosis for the future. In some cases, it may be more humane to euthanize the pet than to allow the pet to suffer. However, this decision can bring with it a lot of guilt. The pet owner did not let nature take its course. In this case, the pet owner had an active role in the ending of the pet's life, which can be difficult to accept.

A Special Bond

When trying to gain independence, a teen sometimes has conflicts with parents and authority figures. This may cause tension between the teen and the rest of the family. Often a teen would much rather spend time with his or her social group than the family. Parents may not be able to understand why their teen no longer wants to spend time at home with the family and why the teen may be working so hard to detach from the family unit. This is normal, and it happens during adolescence as the teen is gaining independence and finding their identity.

During this time, the family pet may be the only ally a teen has in the household. A pet does not care that the teen would rather spend Friday night with friends than playing Scrabble with the family. The pet does not care that the teen wants to be able to stay out until ten o'clock on school nights. As a result, a teen may feel closer to the family pet than to other members of the household during this development period.

Coping With the Loss of a Pet

Grief for the loss of a pet is a real emotion. Here are some tips on dealing with the loss:

Saying goodbye to a pet can be just as painful as experiencing the death of a friend or relative. Pets become part of our families, and they often share the strongest bonds with the youngest family members.

Veterinarians can not only help with your pet's health, but they can also help you through the grieving process. Your vet may be able to direct you to support groups and other organizations.

- Don't let people tell you that your feelings are silly or that you are overreacting to the loss of a pet. You are entitled to your feelings, and it is perfectly natural to be deeply saddened by the loss of a family pet.
- Talk about the pet with people you trust. It can help to express feelings of sadness for the loss of the pet. Keeping these feelings bottled up will only cause more sadness. It is okay to cry.
- Remember the good times with the pet.
- Avoid people who will minimize your feelings of grief for the pet.
- Consider joining a support group for people who have lost pets. There are groups in towns across the country that meet to discuss these issues. There are also online support groups for people grieving the loss of a pet.[3] These are good places to talk to people going through the same loss.
- If necessary, take some time before getting a new pet. People need to process their feelings of grief. If they do not, they may feel resentment toward the new pet. You need to be ready for a new pet to come into your life and your heart.
- When you do feel ready for a new pet, think carefully before choosing one similar to the previous pet. A new and healthy relationship with this new pet needs to be formed. For some people, this may be easier with a pet of a different breed or appearance.

Grieving pet owners should not allow others to belittle their feelings. They should utilize the same support systems that may be needed in the event of the death of a loved one or friend.

It is wise to get one's business affairs in order so surviving loved ones are not burdened with these details while they are grieving their loss.

Preparations

When a person dies, there is a great deal that needs to be done in terms of paperwork, service preparations, memorials, and disposing of the body. Also legal issues about the person's property, businesses, children, and home may arise. It can be overwhelming for those left to deal with sorting out these things. Preparing for death helps alleviate some of the stress associated with these issues. Even if a person is young and healthy, it is important to prepare just in case. This way, their loved ones have less to do upon their death. They won't need to waste time guessing what the wishes of the deceased would be in a given situation.

Planning for Death

For people who have a terminal illness or people who just want to make sure their family members are not left to figure out their wishes, there is a phrase that many use to describe getting everything taken care of so things are settled in the event of their death. It is called getting one's affairs in order. People know that it is not a good sign when they are told by their doctor to get their affairs in order. It means that death is a likely result of the illness or condition they are suffering from or that the illness or condition may cause mental impairment that will leave them no longer able to make decisions on their own.

Now they must make decisions about their finances, their medical care, any young children they may have, their property, and their wishes regarding a funeral or memorial service. With death, there are many details to deal with. Some people would rather avoid this topic entirely. People generally do not want to think about their death, their affairs, or their funeral. Some are even superstitious and think that if they plan for their death, they will die. However, it does help the immediate family left behind. When deceased people have previously made some decisions and gathered documentation that will be needed upon their death, this can lessen the burden on the family. If their wishes are clear and information is readily available, there will be less stress on the family, at least regarding the planning process. Family members do not want to go on a wild goose chase for life insurance information and other related documents when a loved one has died. They are grieving; their concentration is poor. It is a difficult time, and it can be even more stressful if affairs were left in a state of disarray. When people are getting their affairs in order, decisions should be made about the following.

Finances. People should have a Last Will and Testament in place and should make sure that it will accurately reflect their wishes. A will sets forth the deceased's wishes about assets and property. It is also important that this is updated periodically to reflect the current situation in the family. If minor children are now adults or people stated in the will to receive assets are no longer living, the will should be updated. Also, the wishes of the person may have changed over time. An updated will should reflect those wishes.

People may also want to give someone power of attorney, or the authorization to make financial decisions for them if and when they become incapacitated. This way they can rest assured knowing that someone they trust will be making decisions for them if it becomes necessary.

Health care. It is a good idea for people to make their wishes known regarding their choices for their health care. They can achieve this by gathering documents known as advance directives. Do they want to be kept alive on a machine? What if they are not conscious—who will make decisions for them? They could sign a durable power of attorney for health care, which will state who will make decisions if they become incapacitated. They can feel comforted knowing that someone with their best interests at heart is making decisions when they are unable.

Would they want to be resuscitated if their heart stops or they stop breathing? If not, they should sign a do-not-resuscitate order (DNR), which will let those who are taking care of them know they do not want to be revived or receive any other lifesaving treatment. When this order is in place, all medical personnel working with a patient are instructed that they cannot give CPR to the patient or otherwise try to resuscitate the person.

People may want to decide whether they would like to donate organs and tissue upon their death. Many lives are saved every year by donated organs. People can specify which organs they would like to donate, if any. Some states allow people to indicate when they receive their driver's license whether they want to be an organ donor. The license then reflects their wish to donate their organs upon their death.

What about pain management? People also might want to discuss what will happen should doctors give them a specific amount of time left to live. In that event, would they want hospice care? Hospice care is for people who are in the last stages of an illness, such as cancer or heart failure, and wish to be as comfortable as possible during that time. The goal is not to treat the illness but rather to keep

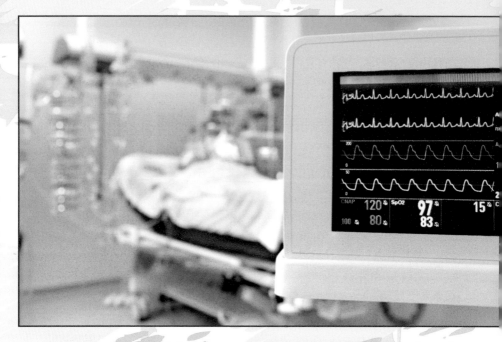

One example of an important preparation consideration is a do-not-resuscitate order, or DNR. No one wants to have to think of such things, but such decisions ultimately help the family.

people comfortable by managing pain and minimizing suffering during their last months. Hospice programs also provide help to the dying person's family. They may provide the family members with literature about the end stages of life and what to expect physically and emotionally from their loved one.

Making these decisions and getting affairs in order while one is still of sound mind and body will not only help the family members who are making plans and arrangements after death, it will also ensure that the deceased's wishes are respected.

Memorials

Once someone has died, a plan needs to be set in motion regarding the disposal of the body and any memorial services planned for the person. It is time to say good-bye to the deceased.

Ritualistic farewells to the dead go back centuries. Every culture pays its respects to the dead in some fashion. Each culture has rituals in which people memorialize the dead while giving them a sacred place to rest for eternity, whether in the earth, above land, or scattered in the form of ashes. The rituals are often rooted in the prevalent religion of the culture. Some cultures believe that death is a new beginning into the beyond, while other cultures see death as the end to an existence and nothing else.

Today many cultures observe visitation, or visiting with the deceased. In Western societies, this usually takes the form of a wake at a funeral home where the body is in either a closed or open casket. The term wake initially described a period of time when loved ones would watch the body of a person before it was buried even during the nighttime hours. Some families use the time during a wake to share stories of the deceased. Often there are prayers offered for the deceased and the bereaved. Friends come to the funeral home to offer comfort to the family. There may be food and drink provided, as this is seen as a celebration of the person's life.

In the Jewish religion, there are periods of mourning after the burial of the deceased. Shiva lasts one week from the date of the burial. During the first three days after the burial, members of the immediate family sit alone and mourn the loss of their loved one. During the last four days of shiva, friends and extended family can visit the immediate family and bring food with them. After shiva, the next period is called sheloshim, which lasts for thirty days after the burial. During this time, the family can resume daily activities, though they continue to mourn, and they may continue to recite the Kaddish prayer every day. After sheloshim, the prayer is recited every Sabbath in the person's honor for twelve months. At this time, close family and friends also visit the gravesite where the grave monument is unveiled. After twelve months, mourning is over except for brief moments on the anniversary of the death, Yarhzeit, according to the Hebrew calendar.

Many people now visit with funeral home directors while they are still alive. They can plan for—and even pay for—the funeral and burial they want without leaving decisions to their family members.

Rituals are ways for people to stay connected to their culture or faith during a time of mourning. Each culture has its own set of rituals, but some rituals transcend many cultures. The ritual of wearing black when mourning has been utilized in many cultures. It garnered a lot of attention in Europe and the United States during the nineteenth century, when widows were expected to dress exclusively in black for the first year. During the second, they could add a bit of black jewelry to their ensemble. During the last six months of mourning, they could introduce colors, such as violet, gray, and white.

Disposition of the Body

Upon death, a body can be buried, cremated, or donated for scientific research. The deceased's body can be buried in a casket in the ground or in a mausoleum above ground. Bodies can also be cremated and the ashes buried, kept in an urn on display, or scattered over land or sea, which is often in an area that was special to the deceased. Burial arrangements can be made before death by the person involved or afterward by the person's family.

Shortly after the death, the person's family usually writes an obituary that will be submitted to the local newspaper to inform the public of the death and also of the life of their loved one. Sometimes, especially for famous people, obituaries are written ahead of time and kept on file to be updated at the time of death.

In addition to deciding on the disposition of the body and what to say in an obituary, family and friends must decide on the type of memorial that would best suit the deceased. If the deceased was part of this discussion prior to his or her death, these decisions are easier to make. If the death was sudden and no preparations were made by the deceased, the family may face stress and turmoil in trying to decide on the appropriate way to honor their loved one.

Each culture has its own traditions and customs regarding funeral services. Some cultures promote the use of a eulogy, or a tribute to the deceased's life. It is often given by someone who was

69

close to the person. Since people may have a hard time reading a eulogy because they are still raw with emotion, it is not uncommon for a person close to the deceased to write the eulogy, which someone else who is less emotional then reads to the people attending the service.

In Orthodox Jewish and Muslim traditions, the funeral and burial are supposed to take place as soon as possible after death—usually within a day—and cremation is forbidden. In Christian churches, practices are more variable.

In some traditions, flowers are sent by family and friends to the funeral home, the church, or the person's home. Often flowers are placed on the grave on special days following the death, such as holidays and the person's birthday. Among Jews, people visiting the grave place a small stone upon it to show they have been there and to honor the dead person. In some cases, the family requests donations in the name of their loved one to a special organization instead of flowers. Donations are sometimes requested for education funds or the needs of minor children if the deceased was a parent. This gives family and friends a way to help those most impacted by the death.

A memorial service may also be held. This differs from a funeral in that the body is not present, and it can be held some time after the death. This is an option if distance of family members or timing is an issue. This way the family is not held to a timeline for disposition of the body, and they can hold the service when important people in the person's life are able to attend.

Healing After Services

After the funeral services and visitors, life will go back to normal in the sense that people will return to their daily activities. Children and teens will go back to school, adults will go back to work, and life and all of its responsibilities will resume. It will now be time for those left behind to adapt to this new life without their loved one.

In the days, weeks, and months after a death, there comes a time when the family will need to decide what to do with the belongings

Planting a memorial tree in honor of someone's life can be a positive way to remember a loved one who has died. As the tree grows, loved ones can remember the person they have lost.

of the deceased. This may be too painful to face right away, so this can occur even years after the death. If the deceased is a child, did the child have his or her own room? If so, what will happen to that room? Should the room be kept as it was when the child was alive? Should the clothes and toys be donated to charity, or should the family keep them because of the memories associated with them? These are all difficult decisions that should not be made in haste.

It can be difficult or awkward to comfort someone who is grieving. It is important to remember that you do not have to do or say anything profound. The person simply needs your comfort.

In the case of the death of an immediate family member, the family may want to discuss this as a group so everyone has input into the decision. One member may feel that holding on to these items is like holding on to the pain. For this person, the items must be disposed of in some way so the family can move on. Another member of the family may fear that memories of this person will fade if they dispose of the belongings. This is a difficult decision for people to make, and each family has to make the best decision for the family as a whole.

Some people who are grieving may also have unfinished business with the deceased. Maybe they have feelings of guilt for something said or not said. Maybe they are seeking a way to channel some of their grief into an activity that helps them. There are many ways that people who are grieving can stay connected to the deceased while still working through their grief process.

Writing. Writing can be an effective tool for people who are dealing with grief. It may help take some of the burden off people who are mourning if they write a letter to the loved one or friend saying the things that they wished they had said when the person was alive.

Journaling can also be very helpful. People can write down their feelings and be sure that they will not be judged on their thoughts. A journal is a place where people can feel safe pouring out their heart on paper. It can be a cathartic experience for those grieving a loved one or friend.

Art. Creating a photo album, memory book, or collage in tribute to the person who has died can be helpful for many people. Such art can include stories about the person and things that made that person special. Today, many younger people create Web sites in honor of their lost loved ones or friends. This way others can visit the site and feel a sense of comfort knowing that the person is not forgotten. An article entitled "You Don't Defriend the Dead: An Analysis of Grief Communication by College Students Through Facebook Profiles" in the journal *Death Studies* looked at research regarding how college students on Facebook interact with the Facebook page of a friend who died. It found that Facebook friends of the deceased maintained their connection through the site. They found it helpful to look at pictures of their friend and even wrote messages on their wall as a way to cope with the loss.[1]

For younger children, a memory bear may be something that will help provide comfort. This is a teddy bear made out of something that once belonged to the deceased, such as clothes or a favorite blanket. It allows the child to feel close to the person. Some children and adults are comforted by quilts made from the clothing of their loved one.

Growth. Some people opt to plant a tree or a garden in honor of the deceased. They watch it grow year after year, which helps them feel that the spirit of the person lives on.

Giving. Some people enjoy participating in events that benefit certain charities or organizations. If the loved one or friend has died from an illness for which research funds are being raised, people may want to raise funds for the group by participating in charity races or other events. They are able to meet others affected by the illness and feel as though they are doing something to help fight the illness or condition.

Often people donate money in honor of the deceased. Donations may be made to the hospital or hospice agency that helped the deceased, a scholarship fund for the deceased's children, or to bring about advances in curing the illness that caused the death.

Giving Comfort

Sometimes when people are trying to comfort someone who is grieving, they find themselves at a loss for words. Other times they are not at a loss for words at all, but they don't have the right words. People who are grieving are not helped by hearing things such as, "You can always remarry" or "You are still young, you can have another child." If you don't know what to say, just say that you are so sorry for their loss. Saying something simple is better than saying something inappropriate.

In her book *How Can I Help: How to Support Someone Who Is Grieving,* June Cerza Kolf warns against using clichés. She offers some suggestions on phrases to avoid and more appropriate responses to use instead:

What Not to Say	What to Say Instead
Time heals everything.	You must feel as if this pain will never end.
Try to look for the good in this situation.	This is just too painful to bear.
Your loved one is better off.	Your loved one is no longer suffering, but I know you certainly are.
The Lord never gives us more than we can handle.	This must be so very hard for you.
Try not to cry.	It is okay to cry. Cry as much as you need to.
I know just how you feel.	I can't even imagine how you must feel. Just know how much I care.
Everything will be okay.	Please let me help however I can.
Let me know if I can do anything.	I'll call tomorrow to see how I can help.[2]

Both before and after death, there are ways for the family and friends of those who are grieving to help. They can help out by getting affairs in order, offering support, and just letting their loved ones know that they are available and ready to listen and help at any time. Reaching out to the grieving person is important. They may not be up to reaching out to others, so it is up to friends and family to reach out to them.

A simple gesture, such as writing a sympathy note, can make all the difference when a friend's loved one has passed away. These notes will be a source of comfort even long after the loved one's death.

Seeking Support

As has been discussed in each chapter in this book, support is key during the grieving process. The support can be from friends, family, church members, coworkers, or even strangers who are grieving. With each loss, there is an emotional response. Also as discussed previously, the nature of the relationship with the deceased, the closeness of the bond, the type of death, and whether it was sudden or prolonged all impact the grief process. Each situation is unique, which makes it difficult to apply a rigid set of standards to the grief process. This is why research is necessary in this field, so trends and responses can be analyzed. This will help medical practitioners and mental health professionals better assess the needs of the grieving. As covered earlier, social media has impacted the grieving process. People feel some comfort in posting to the Facebook wall of their deceased friends. This is a new phenomenon that was only made possible by changes in technology over the past twenty years.

Also, people are living longer due to technology and advancements in the medical field. As a result, more research should focus on the elderly, dementia, and grief. Grief research is always expanding, and it is very important, as each person will likely encounter a loss in their lifetime.

Long-Term Impact of Loss

Some people may learn to get past the grief eventually, but for others the death of a loved one has changed their lives forever. The person who has died was a part of them in life, and many people want to keep it that way even after the death. People who are grieving experience many reactions, some of which are expected and some unexpected. Knowing that some reactions are common may be helpful for people who are in the process of grieving.

Since the body and mind are interconnected, there are physical, behavioral, mental, spiritual, and emotional reactions associated with grief. It is important to be aware of these changes so people can recognize them in loved ones and friends but also in themselves. Mary Ann Emswiler and James Emswiler, in their book *Guiding Your Child Through Grief*, compiled the following list of reactions that younger people may experience in response to death.

Emotional Reactions
- Crying, weepiness
- Hiding grief
- Being easily startled
- Loneliness

Behavioral Reactions
- Sexually acting out
- Risky behavior
- Restlessness
- Withdrawal
- Clingy behavior, not wanting to be alone
- Regression back to habits of younger years

- Reacting to stress
- Less productive in schoolwork
- Avoiding reminders of the person who died

Mental Reactions

- Problems with concentration
- Boredom
- Absentmindedness
- Lack of interest in hobbies or school

Spiritual Reactions

- Dreams and paranormal experiences during which the person dreams of the deceased person or feels his or her presence

Physical Reactions

- Change in appetite
- Fatigue
- Physical complaints and physical weakness
- Headaches
- Stomachaches
- Change in sleeping habits[1]

Many of these are normal reactions to grief. However, family members and friends must continue to observe the grieving person to see if any of these reactions seem to be more severe. For example, has the weepiness and sadness turned into suicidal thoughts? Has a tendency for the person to withdraw turned into complete isolation? Has the person turned to drugs and alcohol to feel better? Often grieving people feel like they are the only person on earth going through such pain. They may look around and see people going about their everyday lives, eating dinner, playing ball, and catching the bus, and they may wonder, "Why am I the only person who feels so incredibly sad?" or "Do these people have any idea how terrible I feel right now? No! They are smiling and having fun while I feel absolutely awful inside." This type of thinking can sink people further into despair.

Those who are grieving often forget to care for themselves. People who want to help can bring food, buy groceries, clean house, and do laundry for the grieving person.

What Can You Do?

Here are some things people can do to help friends or family members during this difficult time:

Listening. If grieving people want to talk about the deceased person, then share a story about the person they are grieving if possible. It can be a funny story or just something silly the person used to do. If they would rather discuss other subjects, let them. Whether it is about sports, their feelings, or school, talk with them about whatever seems to help at the moment. Listening can be an effective tool in helping someone who is grieving.

Accepting. Understand that grieving people have suffered a loss that might change them in some ways forever. People learn to live with loss but may be a little different from then on, as a piece of them is now missing. Accept them even if they are changed in some ways forever.

Don't take any declined invitation as a rejection. Friends or family members who are grieving may not be ready to go out and enjoy the same things they used to—at least not right away. Don't take it personally. People move back into day-to-day activities at their own pace. Give them space if they need it. Be attentive to their needs. If they desire company and support, be sure to continue to act as you have always acted; if you usually call them every day, continue to do so if they are open to that. If they are not up to speaking, most likely they will let you know. Don't avoid a grieving person because it feels awkward.

Writing. Send your friend a note expressing your condolences, or write a letter or poem about the person he or she is grieving. Buy a card that expresses how you feel. Many bereaved people save such notes and find comfort in them long after they are sent.

Helping. Offer to help out with chores around the house, errands, or anything your friend might need a hand with. During a time of grief, it can be difficult for a person to keep up with day-to-day tasks that need to be taken care of.

81

Help Is Available

When people are grieving, especially if this is the first time they have lost a loved one or friend, some emotions, experiences, and reactions from others might be unexpected and, as a result, evoke more emotion. It might help to know that certain situations can trigger emotional reactions. Understanding that there will be good days and bad days is important. Important dates, such as birthdays and holidays, may be difficult, and that is okay. If an important person is gone, it is normal to feel that loss even for years to come. For some people, holidays and momentous events trigger sadness. For others, it is the period leading up to the event that triggers strong emotion.

With the sadness and pain that some people experience as the result of the death of a loved one or friend, they may be tempted to self-medicate. Grieving people should avoid the temptation to use drugs or alcohol to numb pain. This may only cause more problems. It is also important for people to not forget to take care of themselves physically. They should try to get enough rest, eat well, and take care of their body. This can become difficult because eating and sleeping habits often change during a time of immense grief. However, when the body begins to break down and become weak, this can exacerbate any emotional issues the person is already going through at the time.

It is okay to express emotions. If a grieving person is angry, that is okay. If he or she is crying, that is okay, and if he or she is not crying, that is okay, too. Just because others are handling loss in a certain way doesn't mean that everyone has to have the same responses. Each person grieves in his or her own way at different times.

Many people grieving the loss of a loved one are devastated. Sometimes they need help working through these emotions but are fearful that others will think they are crazy if they seek the help of outside resources. Grieving is just one of the many reasons a person can seek the help of mental health professionals and support services. It does not mean that the person is crazy or mentally ill; it

Famous Quotes on Grief

To weep is to make less the depth of grief.
—William Shakespeare

There is no pain so great as the memory of joy in present grief.
—Aeschylus

I hold it true, whate'er befall;
I feel it, when I sorrow most;
'Tis better to have loved and lost
Than never to have loved at all.
—From "In Memoriam A.H.H.,"
Alfred, Lord Tennyson

just means that he or she is looking for support during this time of grief and pain.

Counseling

In his book *Grief Counseling and Grief Therapy: A Handbook for the Mental Health Professional,* J. William Worden, Ph.D., distinguishes between grief therapy and grief counseling. He reserves grief therapy for situations in which there is an abnormal or complicated grief reaction.[2] Grief counseling, he states, helps people with uncomplicated normal grief.[3] If someone seems to be suffering from complicated grief, therapy with a professional may be warranted.

There are some things that distinguish grief therapy from grief counseling. Grief therapy is generally more structured, often done in a one-on-one setting, and led by a trained professional in the field of grief and bereavement.[4] Grief counseling, on the other hand, is less structured, done in a group setting or private setting, and can be facilitated by someone without specific training in grief and bereavement.[5] The intensity and duration of a person's reactions will determine whether there is a need for grief counseling or grief therapy.

Community Support

Teens may feel comfortable around other teens, so one place that may be comforting is a local support group for teens dealing with the loss of a loved one. Peers can look to each other for support. Although the loss may be different for each teen, the other issues involved with being a teenager are the same. It may help to talk with people of the same age and in the same community who are going through the same thing.

Contacting the local mental health association to see if it could provide a list of groups in the area is a good place to start. Teens can also look online. Many places that offer support counseling have Web sites. There are also Web-based support groups in which people communicate strictly online. This type of support system may help some people, but others may need the physical support from the group, such as hugs and activities done during the group meetings that help with grief. Also, religious organizations, local hospitals, and facilities that provide hospice care may have a list of counseling support groups in the area.

The teen might also want to set up an appointment with a private grief therapist for a one-on-one session. This type of talk therapy can be helpful for people going through a crisis. Be sure to specify the need to speak with a bereavement therapist—someone skilled and trained specifically in providing therapy to those who are grieving and those who may be having complicated grief reactions.

People can also go to their church and speak with a member of the clergy about their feelings. When someone dies, people sometimes have questions about their faith. Talking to a clergyperson can help those who are looking for spiritual guidance.

Death is one of the hardest things any of us ever has to deal with. Don't feel that you have to go through it alone. Professionals, such as doctors and counselors, are available to help you cope.

Cherishing the Memories

Working through grief emotions can be difficult. For many people, the grief will subside, but the loss will be with them forever. Understanding the emotions involved in the grief process and discussing how life changes as the result of the death of a loved one are important in understanding the journey ahead. For many people, the death of a loved one is one of the most difficult times in their lives. But with the support of friends, family, and professionals, they will get through it.

Sigmund Freud, a pioneer in the field of psychiatry, described how feelings of grief may subside over time but how the loss can become a part of the grieving person. In a letter dated April 12, 1929, to his friend and colleague Ludwig Binswanger, Freud wrote about the feelings he experienced after the death of his daughter, Sophie. Sophie would have been thirty-six on the day the letter was written. She had died in 1920 at twenty-six years of age from complications related to the Spanish flu. In his letter to his friend, Freud wrote:

> Although we know that after such a loss the acute state of mourning will subside, we also know we shall remain inconsolable and will never find a substitute. No matter what may fill the gap, even if it be filled completely, it nevertheless remains something else. And actually this is how it should be. It is the only way of perpetuating that love which we do not want to relinquish.[6]

As seen from the research discussed in this book, dealing with loss is difficult. Feelings of emptiness, fear, anger, and sadness are just some of the emotions people may experience in the aftermath of a loss. Life also changes in some ways due to the death of a loved one. The memories of those loved ones can be kept alive by talking about the person and sharing their stories. It also important to focus energy on people who are still here. This can be done by putting effort into friendships and family relationships. Spending time with friends and family, reaching out to them, or just telling them they are care for and appreciated are all ways to show a person you care for them. Even after a loved one's death, you can show your feelings for them by not forgetting them and keeping their memory alive by talking about them and sharing their special qualities with others.

Chapter Notes

Chapter 1: Everyone Experiences Loss

1. *Austin Child Guidance Center,* n.d., <http://www. austinchildguidance.org/for-parents/parenting-articles-tips/grief-and-loss-when-your-child-loses-someone-close/> (February 18, 2015).

Chapter 2: Grief's Impact

1. "Major Depressive Disorder and the 'Bereavement Exclusion,'" *American Psychiatric Association,* 2013, <http://www.dsm5.org/ Documents/Bereavement%20Exclusion%20Fact%20Sheet.pdf> (March 2, 2015).

2. US Department of Justice, "Amber Alert," *Office of Justice Programs,* January 2010, <http://ojp.gov/newsroom/pdfs/amberchronology. pdf> (March 2, 2015).

3. William Worden, *Grief Counseling and Grief Therapy: A Handbook for the Mental Health Professional, 3rd Edition* (New York, N.Y.: Springer Publishing Company, 2001), p. 27.

4. Worden, p. 32.

5. Ibid., p. 37.

6. Alan D. Wolfelt, *Understanding Grief: Helping Yourself Heal* (New York, N. Y.: Routledge, 1992), pp. 135–142.

7. Melhem, Nadine, Giovanna Porta, Monica Walker Payne, and David Brent. "Identifying Prolonged Grief Reactions in Children: Dimensional and Diagnostic Approaches," *Journal of the American Academy of Child and Adolescent Psychiatry,* vol. 52, no. 6, 2013, pp. 599–607.

8. Worden, p. 10.

9. Ibid.

10. Ibid., p. 12.

Chapter 3: The Loss of Someone Close

1. Allison Werner-Lin, Ph.D., LCSW, and Nancee M. Biank, LCSW. "Holding Parents So They Can Hold Their Children: Grief Work with Surviving Spouses to Support Parentally Bereaved Children," *Omega*, vol. 66, no. 1, pp. 2012–2013.

2. Ibid., p. 11.

3. Angela Nickerson, Richard A. Bryant, Idan M. Aderka, Devon E. Hinton, and Stefan G. Hofmann. "The Impacts of Parental Loss and Adverse Parenting on Mental Health: Findings From the National Comorbidity Survey-Replication," *Psychological Trauma: Theory, Research, Practice, and Policy,* vol. 5, no. 2, 2013, pp. 119–127.

Chapter 4: Changing Family Dynamic

1. Barbara D Rosof, *The Worst Loss: How Families Heal From the Death of a Child* (New York, N.Y.: Henry Holt and Company, 1994), p. 33.

2. Ibid., p. 32.

3. Holly B. Herberman Mash, Ph.D., Carol S. Fullerton, Ph.D., and Robert J. Ursano, M.D. "Complicated Grief and Bereavement in Young Adults Following Close Friend and Sibling Loss," *Depression and Anxiety,* vol. 30, 2013, pp. 1202–1210.

Chapter 5: First Grief Experience

1. Carla Ens and John B. Bonds Jr. "Death Anxiety and Personal Growth in Adolescents Experiencing the Death of a Grandparent" *Death Studies,* vol. 29, 2005, pp. 171–178.

2. "Grandparents Day 2012: Sept. 9," *US Census Bureau News,* July 21, 2012, <http://www.census.gov/newsroom/releases/pdf/cb12ff-17_grandparents.pdf> (July 31, 2012).

3. "Cognitive Impairment: A Call For Action Now!" *Centers for Disease Control and Prevention,* February 2011, <http://www.cdc.gov/aging/pdf/cognitive_impairment/cogimp_poilicy_final.pdf> (March 1, 2015).

4. Ibid.

5. Caitlin K. Holley, Ph.D and Benjamin T. Mast, Ph.D., "Predictors of Anticipatory Grief in Dementia Caretakers," *Clinical Gerontologist,* vol. 33, 2010, pp. 223–236.

Chapter 6: Death of a Young Person

1. Arialdi M. Miniño, "Mortality Among Teenagers Aged 12–19 Years: United States, 1999–2006," *NCHS Data Brief, Centers for Disease Control and Prevention,* no. 37, May 2010, <http://www.cdc.gov/nchs/data/databriefs/db37.pdf> (March 2, 2015).

2. "Teen Drivers – Additonal Resources," *National Highway Traffic Safety Administration,* n.d., <http://www.nhtsa.gov/Driving+Safety/Teen+Drivers/Teen+Drivers+-+Additional+Resources> (March 2, 2015).

3. Tammy LaGorce, "Confronting Prom Night Drinking," *New York Times,* June 1, 2008, <http://www.nytimes.com/2008/06/01/nyregion/nyregionspecial2/01Rproms.html> (June 18, 2008).

4. Miniño.

5. "Suicide and Self Inflicted Injury," *Centers for Disease Control and Prevention,* February 6, 2015,<http://www.cdc.gov/nchs/fastats/suicide.htm> (March 2, 2015).

6. "Suicide in the U.S.: Statistics and Prevention," *National Institute of Mental Health,* n.d., <http://www.nimh.nih.gov/health/

publications/suicide-in-the-us-statistics-and-prevention.shtml> (June 18, 2008).

7. "Bullied Girl's Suicide Has Ongoing Impact," *NBC News,* December 28, 2011, <http://usnews.nbcnews.com/_ news/2011/12/28/9781587-bullied-girls-suicide-has-ongoing-impact?lite> (March 2, 2015).

Chapter 7: Pets Are Family Too

1. "What I Know for Sure," *O, The Oprah Magazine,* August 2007, <http://www.oprah.com/omagazine/200708/omag_200708_ mission.jhtml> (July 29, 2007).

2. Ibid.

3. Petloss.com, <http://petloss.com> (March 2, 2015).

Chapter 8: Preparations

1. Natalie Pennington. "You Don't Defriend the Dead: An Analysis of Grief Communication by College Students Through Facebook Profiles." *Death Studies,* vol. 37, 2013, pp. 617–635.

2. June Cerza Kolk, *How Can I Help: How to Support Someone Who Is Grieving* (Cambridge, Mass.: DaCapo Press, 1991), pp. 11–12.

Chapter 9: Seeking Support

1. Mary Ann Emswiler and James P. Emswiler, *Guiding Your Child Through Grief* (New York, N.Y.: Bantam Books, 2000), p. 38.

2. J. William Worden, *Grief Counseling and Grief Therapy: A Handbook for the Mental Health Professional, 3rd Edition* (New York, N.Y.: Springer Publishing Company, 2001), p. 51.

3. Ibid.

4. Brook Noel and Pamela D. Blair, *I Wasn't Ready to Say Goodbye: Surviving, Coping, and Healing After the Sudden Death of a Loved One*

(Naperville, Ill.: Sourcebooks, Inc., 2008), pp. 220–221.

5. Ibid.

6. Sigmund Freud, *Letters of Sigmund Freud, Reprint Edition* (Mineola, New York: Dover Publications, 1992), p. 386.

Glossary

advance directive—Legal documentation stating the care and treatment that a person will receive should he or she become unable to make decisions affecting his or her health.

Alzheimer's disease—A progressive neurological disease of the brain that leads to dementia.

anticipatory grief—Grief that occurs when a person is expecting a loss.

apathy—A lack of interest or concern or a lack of emotion or feeling.

bereavement—A state of sadness, mourning, and grief after a loved one has died.

bickering—Fighting about insignificant things.

burial—The ritual of placing a corpse in a grave.

cognition—Mental processing that involves awareness, perception, reasoning, and judgment.

cremation—The process of incinerating a dead body.

cyberbullying—Using electronic communication to bully a person by sending messages of an intimidating or harassing nature.

dementia—Deterioration of intellectual faculties, such as memory, concentration, and judgment resulting from an organic disease or a disorder of the brain.

depression—An illness involving both the body and mind in which a person has changes in eating and sleeping habits, as well as concentration. A person may feel sad and have a loss of interest in activities once enjoyed.

despair—Loss of hope.

do-not-resuscitate order (DNR)—Instructions ordering medical personnel not to administer life-sustaining treatment on a person.

durable power of attorney for health care—A written advance directive in which a person names an agent who will make decisions regarding health care and treatment in the event that the patient cannot make his or her own decisions.

euthanize—To end a life in the most painless way possible.

guilt—Remorse caused by a feeling that one has done something wrong.

hospice—A facility that provides special care for people who have less than six months to live, where a focus is placed on comfort, not treatment.

intermittent explosive disorder—Repeated episodes of impulsive, aggressive, angry, or violent behavior, statements, or actions where the reaction is not in proportion to the event.

Kaddish—A prayer recited in daily synagogue services and by Jewish mourners after the death of a close relative.

magical thinking—Nonscientific reasoning that includes such ideas as connections between unrelated events and the mind's ability to affect the physical world.

mausoleum—A large burial chamber that is usually above ground.

paranoia—Distrust of others and things, which is not based on rational thought.

power of attorney—The legal authority to act on another's behalf.

sheloshim—Including the seven days of shiva, this is the thirty-day period after the burial of a family member in the Jewish faith.

shiva—Mourning period in the Jewish faith of seven days after the death of a close relative.

will—A legal document that declares the wishes of a deceased person regarding their assets.

Yahrzeit—In the Jewish faith, the anniversary of the death of a relative.

yearning—Deep longing.

For More Information

Alzheimer's Association National Office

225 N. Michigan Ave., Fl. 17

Chicago, IL 60601

1-800-272-3900

alz.org

American Association of Suicidology

5221 Wisconsin Avenue, NW

Washington, D.C. 20015

202-237-228

suicidology.org

American Childhood Cancer Organization

10920 Connecticut Ave.

Suite A

Kensington MD 20895

855-858-2226

acco.org

American Trauma Society

201 Park Washington

Court Falls Church, VA 22046

800-556-7890

amtrauma.org

Children's Cancer Association

1200 NW Naito Parkway, Suite 140

Portland, OR 97209

503-244-3141

joyrx.org

Compassionate Friends, Inc., National Headquarters
1000 Jorie Blvd. Suite 140
Oak Brook, IL 60523
630-990-0010
compassionatefriends.org/home.aspx

Kids in Crisis
1 Salem Street
Cos Cob, CT 06807
203-327-5437
kidsincrisis.org

The National Center for Grieving Children and Families
PO Box 86852
Portland, OR 97286
866-775-5683
dougy.org

National Alliance for Grieving Children
900 SE Ocean Blvd.
Suite 130D
Stuart, FL 34994
866-432-1542
nationalallianceforgrievingchildren.org

National Hospice and Palliative Care Organization
1731 King Street
Alexandria, Virginia 22314
703-837-1500
nhpco.org

Web Sites

aplb.org

The Association for Pet Loss and Bereavement helps people cope with the loss of a beloved animal.

fernside. org

Fernside provides grief support, outreach, and education to families, as well as the community.

griefnet.org

Find support by connecting with others who are dealing with grief and loss.

kidsaid.com

Children can share feelings through an e-mail support group, share stories and artwork, and find answers to their questions.

teenline.com

A teen-to-teen hotline with community outreach services.

yellowribbon.org

The Yellow Ribbon Suicide Prevention Program has a hotline to call if someone is contemplating suicide, discusses how to recognize warning signs, provides a schedule of training sessions, and more.

Further Reading

Grollman, Earl A. *Talking About Death: A Dialogue Between Parent and Child.* Boston, Mass.: Beacon Press, 2011.

Kornfeld, Jody. *Death and Bereavement.* New York, N.Y.: Rosen Publishing Group, 2012.

Scarff, Susan Kiser, and Ann Kiser Zultner. *Dementia: The Journey Ahead—A Practical Guide for In-Home Caregivers.* Minneapolis, Minn.: Langdon Street Press, 2012.

Wolfelt, Alan. *Companioning the Grieving Child: A Soulful Guide for Caregivers (The Companioning Series.)* Chicago, Ill.: Companion Press, 2012.

Wolfelt, Alan. *Finding the Words: How to Talk With Children and Teens About Death, Suicide, Homicide, Funerals, Cremation, and Other End-of-Life Matters.* Chicago, Ill.: Companion Press, 2013.

Index

20–21, 24, 37, 39–40, 45,
50–52
developmental level and
grieving, 25, 29
disorganization and despair
stage, 21
do-not-resuscitate order
(DNR), 65
drug abuse, 31, 50–52, 79, 82

E

emotional relocation, 23
eulogies, 69–70
euthanasia of pets, 58

F

family unit
grandparent's place in, 13, 42,
44
sibling loss effects, 36, 38
flowers, 70
Freud, Sigmund, 86
friend, loss of
drug/alcohol abuse, 49–52
motor vehicle accidents,
49–50
peer reaction to, 8, 10, 40, 50,
54–55, 74, 77, 82
school violence, 51–52, 54
suicide, 52, 54–55
funerals, 10, 13, 20, 64, 67,
69–70

G

getting one's affairs in order, 64,
66, 75
grandparent, loss of

adolescents and, 14, 41,
44–46, 49
family relationships, 13, 42,
44
grandchild's reactions to, 44,
46
illness and grief, 44–45
as parental figure, 42, 44
grief therapy/counseling, 36,
83–84
grieving process
acceptance, 16, 20
bargaining, 16, 18
belongings, disposal of,
70–73
charitable donations, 18, 72,
74
denial, 13, 16, 20, 23, 44–45
depression, 10, 15–16, 18,
20–21, 24, 37, 39–40, 45,
50–52
disorganization and despair,
21
illness, 10, 16, 18, 44–45,
63–65, 74
Kübler-Ross stages, 18, 20
memory bears, 74
normal versus complicated,
23–24, 39–40, 83–84
numbness, 20
overview, 16, 18, 20–21, 23
reorganization, 21
tasks, 21, 23, 25
writing/journaling, 73
guilt as reaction, 13, 21, 23, 25,
31, 33, 37, 39, 54–55, 58, 73

surviving spouse reactions,
   28–29, 33–34

T

"The Widower," 12

W

wakes, 67
wills, 64
Winfrey, Oprah, 57
Wolfelt, Alan D., 23–24
Worden, J. William, 21, 23, 25,
   83
writing/journaling, 73, 81

Y

yearning, 21, 46